God Uses Kids Too!

Frankye Derrick

AuthorHouse™
1663 Liberty Drive
Bloomington, IN 47403
www.authorhouse.com
Phone: 1-800-839-8640

All scriptures are taken from the New King James Version Copyright 1992 by Thomas Nelson.

© 2012 Frankye Derrick. All Rights Reserved.

No part of this book may be reproduced, stored in a retrieval system, or transmitted by any means without the written permission of the author.

Published by AuthorHouse 09/24/2012

ISBN: 978-1-4772-7337-1 (sc)
          978-1-4772-7338-8 (e)

Any people depicted in stock imagery provided by Thinkstock are models, and such images are being used for illustrative purposes only. Certain stock imagery © Thinkstock.

This book is printed on acid-free paper.

Because of the dynamic nature of the Internet, any web addresses or links contained in this book may have changed since publication and may no longer be valid. The views expressed in this work are solely those of the author and do not necessarily reflect the views of the publisher, and the publisher hereby disclaims any responsibility for them.

God Uses Kids Too!

By
Frankye Derrick

This book is dedicated to my beautiful grandchildren.

God the Help of Those Who Seek Him

I will lift up my eyes to the hills from whence comes my help? My help comes from the Lord, Who made heaven and earth. He will not allow my foot to be moved; He who keeps me will not slumber. Because He who keeps Israel shall neither slumber not sleep. The Lord is my keeper; the Lord is my shade at my right hand. The sun shall not strike me by day, nor the moon by night. The Lord shall preserve me from all evil; He shall preserve my soul. The Lord shall preserve my going out and my coming in from this time forth and even forevermore.   Psalm 121

A Psalm of Thanksgiving

Make a joyful shout to the Lord, all you lands! Serve the Lord with gladness; come before His presence with singing. Know that the Lord, He is God. It is He who has made us and not we ourselves. We are His people and the sheep of His pasture. Enter into His gates with thanksgiving and into His courts with praise. Be thankful to Him and bless His name . For the Lord is good, His mercy is everlasting and His truth endures to all generations. Psalm 100

LOVE

Love suffers long and is kind; love does not envy; love does not parade itself; is not puffed up; does not behave rudely; does not seek its own; is not provoked; thinks no evil; does not rejoice in iniquities; but rejoices in the truth; bears all things; believes all things; hopes all things, endures all things. Love never fails

1 Corinthians 13:4-8

Trust in the Lord with all your heart and lean not on your own understanding; in all your ways acknowledge Him and He shall direct your path.   Proverbs 3:5, 6

⁵ Now hope does not disappoint, because the love of God has been poured out in our hearts by the Holy Spirit who was given to us.   Romans 5:5

Yet in all these things we are more than conquerors through Him who loved us. For I am persuaded that neither death nor life, nor angels nor principalities nor powers nor things present nor things to come nor height nor depth nor any other created thing, shall be able to separate us from the love of God which is in Christ Jesus our Lord.   Romans 8:37-39

Children

Children, obey your parents in the Lord, for this is right. 2 "Honor your father and mother," which is the first commandment with promise: 3 "that it may be well with you and you may live long on the earth."   Ephesians 6:1-3

Hear, my children, the instruction of a father, And give attention to know understanding; Proverbs 4:1

But you *are* a chosen generation, a royal priesthood, a holy nation, His own special people, that you may proclaim the praises of Him who called you out of darkness into His marvelous light; 1 Peter 2:9

But seek first the kingdom of God and His righteousness and all these things shall be added to you. Matthew 6:33

Whatever things you ask when you pray believe that you receive them and you shall have them. Mark 11:24

Parents

And you, fathers, do not provoke your children to wrath, but bring them up in the training and admonition of the Lord.   Ephesians 6:4

Train up a child in the way he should go and when he is old he will not depart from it. Proverbs 22:6

Foolishness is bound up in the heart of a child; the rod of correction will drive it far from him. Proverbs 22:15

Do not withhold correction from a child. For if you beat him with a rod he will not die. You shall beat him with a rod and deliver his soul from hell.   Proverbs 23:13,14

Children's children are the crown of old men, And the glory of children is their father. Proverbs 17:6

He who spares the rod hates his son but he who loves him disciplines him promptly. Proverbs 13:24

All your children shall be taught by the Lord and great shall be the peace of your children. Isaiah 5:13

God prepared a table before us fill with everything we need. Love, joy, peace, prosperity, health, wealth, long life

Psalm 23:5
You prepare a table before me in the presence of my enemies; You anoint my head with oil; My cup runs over.

He who did not spare His own Son but gave Him up for us all, how can He not with Him freely give us all things.   Hebrews 8:32

Now unto Him who is able to do exceedingly, abundantly above all that we dare ask or think according to the power that works in us.   Ephesians 3:2

Introduction

Children need to learn how to confess the word of God and use it in their own lives. They can show their friends that God needs to be a part of their lives as well as in their parent lives. Parents, read these stories to your children and help them say the confessions everyday it will make a difference in their young lives. It is never too early or they are never too young to start confessing the word of God. The younger the better then they will know how to confess the word over themselves when they need to. They can live a victorious life with Jesus as their Lord and Savior at a young age. They can overcome peer pressure, temptation, shyness and rebellion by confessing the Word of God every day. Confessing the word everyday with your child is the best thing you can do for them or give them. It prepares them for life, it helps them to learn how to hear from God and obey what He is telling them to do. They will know what their purpose in life is by confessing the word and spending time with God through prayer. They will know that God is real as they confess His word and see what they say come to pass. They handle problems, situations and circumstances in a different way because they will confess the positive word over themselves. They will know that God is always with them no matter what.

Know who you are in Christ by meditating and studying the word of God. Say the word of God to yourself everyday, all day so you can see yourself the way God sees you.

I am made in the image and likeness of God.   Genesis 1:27

Before I formed you in the womb I knew you. Before you were born I sanctified you; I ordained you a prophet to the nations.   Jeremiah 1:5

I will praise thee; for I am fearfully and wonderfully made; marvelous are thy works and that my soul know right well. My substance was not hid from thee, when I was made in secret and curiously wrought in the lowest parts of the earth. Thine eyes did see my substance yet being unperfect and in thy book all my members were written, which in continuance were fashioned who as yet there was none of them.   Psalm 139:14

Be like a tree rooted and grounded its roots digs deep down into the ground. So when a strong wind comes it can't blow it down because the tree is strong and rooted deep down into the ground. You can be the same way with the word of God have the word rooted deep into you by saying the word everyday and believe what you say is so. So when problems comes your way you want be knock down. You can be strong in the Lord and in the power of His might.   Ephesians 6:10-18

Finally, my brethren, be strong in the Lord and in the power of His might. [11] Put on the whole armor of God, that you may be able to stand against the wiles of the devil. [12] For we do not wrestle against flesh and blood, but against principalities, against powers, against the rulers of the darkness of this age,[a] against spiritual hosts of wickedness in the heavenly places. [13] Therefore take up the whole armor of God, that you may be able to withstand in the evil day, and having done all, to stand.[14] Stand therefore, having girded your waist with truth, having put on the breastplate of righteousness, [15] and having shod your feet with the preparation of the gospel of peace; [16] above all, taking the shield of faith with which you will be able to quench all the fiery darts of the wicked one. [17] And take the helmet of salvation, and the sword of the Spirit, which is the word of God; [18] praying always with all prayer and supplication in the Spirit, being watchful to this end with all perseverance and supplication for all the saints—

The words you speak can make your life good or bad, happy or sad, rich or poor it is up to you. Speak what God speaks about you and make your life what God says.

This book of the Law shall not depart from your mouth but you shall meditate in it day and night that you may observe to do according to all that is written in it. For then you will make your way prosperous and then you will have good success.   Joshua 1:8

But his delight is in the law of the Lord and in His law he meditate day and night. He shall be like a tree planted by the rivers of water that brings forth the fruit in its season. Whose leaf also shall not wither and whatever he does shall prosper.   Psalm 1:2, 3

For the word of God is living and powerful and sharper than any two-edged sword piercing even to the division of soul and spirit and of joints and marrow and is a discerner of the thoughts and intents of the heart.   Hebrews 4:12

My son, give attention to my words incline your ear to my sayings. Do not let them depart from your eyes; keep them in the midst of your heart. For they are life to those who find them and health to all their flesh.   Proverbs 4:20-22

Pleasant words are like a honeycomb. Sweetness to the soul and health to the bones. Proverbs 16:24

A man's stomach shall be satisfied from the fruit of his mouth. From the produce of his lips he shall be filled. Death and life are in the power of the tongue and those who love it will eat its fruit. Proverbs 18:20, 21

Over Coming Fear

Will is spending a night over Alonzo's house tonight. He was excited about going because Alonzo always talks about God. Will is afraid when he is in the dark by himself. Alonzo said you don't have to be afraid because God is always with you where ever you go. God lives in you and He will protect you from harm. Nothing will harm you if you believe God is on your side. Will always felt good when he went to Alonzo's house because they always prayed and he wasn't afraid like he was at home. Will's dad dropped him off at Alonzo's house and Alonzo took him to his room so he could put his clothes in there. Before going to bed they were going to watch a movie and eat some popcorn with Alonzo's dad, mom and sisters. So they watched the movie and ate popcorn now it was time to go to bed. Will was a little nervous because he didn't want to be jumping and talking in his sleep. Alonzo's dad came in the room and they got down on their knees and said a prayer before going to bed.

We thank You, Father, that the blood of Jesus protects us while we sleep. We thank You, that Jesus is always with us so we are not afraid. We lay down and our sleep is sweet and peaceful. We keep our minds on Jesus and we have sweet dreams. The Lord is on our side so we have no fear.   In Jesus' Name!   Amen!

Will was happy when he woke up he slept really good. He didn't have a bad dream or anything. He had a really good dream so he asked Alonzo's dad if he would write down a prayer he could say every night before he went to bed. He didn't want to have any more bad dreams.

Jesus is always with you He will never leave you. Greater is He who is in you than he who is in the world. (1 John 4:4) Jesus lives in you and He is greater than anything you can be afraid of. Jesus is always right there with you; you can't see Him but He is right there with you. His blood protects you from any harm.

Confessions:

God did not give me the spirit of fear, but of power, of love and of a sound mind.
1 Timothy 1:7

The Lord is my light and my salvation; whom shall I fear? The Lord is the strength of my life; of whom shall I be afraid?   Psalm 27:1

When I lay down, I will not be afraid; yes I will lie down and my sleep will be sweet.
Proverbs 3:24

The Lord is on my side. Whom shall I fear? What can man do to me?
Psalm 118:6

The name of th Lord is a strong tower the righteous run to it and are safe.
Proverbs 18:10

People are afraid of all kinds of things spider, bats, bugs, cats, dogs, rats, the dark, snakes, their own shadow. They are afraid to fly, to get on a boat because they are afraid of water. You have to know that Jesus is always with you no matter where you are and He will protect you.

<u>Hebrews 13:5</u>
Let your conduct be without covetousness; be content with such things as you have. For He Himself has said, "I will never leave you nor forsake you."

By Jesus' Stripes WE Were Healed!

    Alonzo, Joe and Will went over to Sylvester's house to see if he could come outside to play. But when they got to his house his Mom said, that he wasn't feeling well and he couldn't come out to play. So Alonzo asked if he could come in and talk to Sylvester. His Mom said yes and told him to come on in. So Alonzo went into Sylvester's room and saw him lying in the bed. He was coughing and sneezing he didn't look good at all. Alonzo told Sylvester about Jesus taking all of his sickness and pain (Matt. 8:17). He told him that the bible says in 1 Peter 2:24 that by Jesus' stripes we were healed. He told him he needed to say to himself that by Jesus' stripes I am healed. Alonzo ask Sylvester was it alright for him to pray for him and Sylvester smiled and said yes. So Alonzo put his hand on Sylvester's head and prayed:

Dear Father God, I thank you for my friend Sylvester. I thank you that Jesus took all of his sickness and pain. I thank You that You sent Your Word and healed him. I thank You that by Jesus' stripes he is healed. I command this sickness to dry up; die and to go right now in Jesus' Name. I thank You, Father that it is done and Sylvester is healed. In Jesus' Name Amen! Alonzo told Sylvester you have to believe that you are healed no matter what it looks like. Even though you still may cough you must believe that you are healed and act like you are healed. So Sylvester sat up in bed talking and laughing with his friends.

Confessions:

By Jesus' stripes I am healed.   1 Peter 2:24
Jesus took all of my sickness and pain.   Matthew 8:17
God sent His word and healed me.   Psalm 107:20
Greater is He who is in me than sickness that is in the world.   1 John 4:4

While we do not look at the things that are seen but at the things are not seen. For the things which are seen are temporary and but the things which are not seen are eternal.

1 Corinthians 4:12

Oh, how I love your law! I meditate on it all day long. Your commands are always with me and make me wiser than my enemies. I have more insight than all my teachers, for I meditate on your statues. I have more understanding than the elders, for I obey your precepts. I have kept my feet from every evil path so that I might obey your word. I have not departed from your laws, for you yourself have taught me. How sweet are your words to my taste, sweeter than honey to my mouth. I gain understanding from your precepts; therefore I hate every wrong path. Your word is a lamp to my feet and a light for my path. I have taken an oath and confirmed it that I will follow your righteous laws.

Psalm 119:97-106

Seek first the Kingdom of God and all these things will be added to you.   Matthew 6:33

I (Jesus) say to you whatever things you ask for when you pray believe that you receive them and you will have them.   Mark 11:24

If you abide in Me and My (Jesus) words abide in you, you will ask what you desire and it will be done for you.   John 15:7

Now this is the confidence we have in Him, that if we ask anything according to His will He hears us. And if we know He hears us whatever we ask we know that we have the petitions that we have asked of Him.   1 John 5:14, 15

Overcomer

For whatever is born of God overcomes the world. And this is the victory that has overcome the world our faith. Who is he who overcomes the world but he who believes that Jesus is the Son of God?   1 John 5;4, 5

You are of God little children and have overcome them because He who is in you is greater than he who is in the world.   1 John 4:4

And they overcame him by the blood of the Lamb (Jesus) and by the word of their testimony. Revelation 12:11

The Spirit Himself bears witness with our spirit that we are children of God. And if children then heirs , heirs of God and joint-heirs with Christ.   Romans 8:16, 17

We are children of God and the blood of Jesus protectes us and it set of free from evil things people do and say. But we have to believe it and say it out loud to ourselves. God gave His Son Jesus to take our punishment for being disobedient. He took all our sickness, all poverty and death for us. We must say what the word of God says everyday and all day long so that it will become real to us. We must believe what the word of God and act like we believe it. We are victorious because Jesus has already won the war for us we just have to believe it.

**But Thanks be to God who gives us the victory through our Lord Jesus Christ.
1 Corinthians 15:57**

Fighting/Bullying

There was a boy at school that kept picking with Sylvester. Sylvester didn't want to tell the teacher because he didn't want the other kids to say he was a cry baby. But he was tried of the boy picking with him everyday. So when the boy said that he was going to beat him up after school. He decided he was going to fight back and beat the boy up. He was nervous and afraid but he was going to fight no matter what. So when school was over and he was heading home the boy was standing in the parking lot waiting on him. So the boy walked up to him and hit him in the face. Sylvester dropped his books and balled his fist up and hit the boy as hard as he could. The boy fell to the ground and Sylvester got down on his knees and just kept hitting him over and over until a man came and stopped the fight. The boy's lip and nose was bleeding from Sylvester hitting him. They had to go to the office and both of them got kicked out of school. Sylvester told his mom he hit me first and I had to protect myself. I don't other kids trying to bully me because they think I am afraid of them. Sylvester's mom said a prayer with him for direction and how to handle problems when they come up without fighting.

Thank You, Father God, for Your protection and Your wisdom to handle bad situations. I am sorry for fighting and I ask for Your forgiveness and I forgive _____ (say the name) help me to take care of this problem in a different way, a good way.   In Jesus' name. Amen!

When a man's ways please the Lord, He makes even his enemies to be at peace with him.
Proverbs 16:7

A false witness will not go unpunished and he who speaks lies will not escape.
Proverbs 19:5

Put on the whole armor of God.
Put on your waist the belt of truth, put on the breastplate of righteousness, cover your feet with the preparation of the gospel of peace, take the shield of faith to quench all the fiery darts that comes from the wicked one, take the helmet of salvation and the sword of the Spirit which is the word of God. Each time you speak the word of God you are cutting up the enemy. When sickness is trying to come on your body and you say "by Jesus' stripes I am healed" you are stopping the sickness. You are cutting it up with the word of God.

For the word of God is living and powerful and sharper than any two-edged sword piercing even to the division of soul and spirit and of joints and marrow and is a discerner of the thoughts and intents of the heart.   Hebrews 4:12

Isaiah 54:17
No weapon formed against you shall prosper, And every tongue which rises againstyou in judgment You shall condemn. This is the heritage of the servants of the LORD, And their righteousness is from **Me**," Says the LORD

Forgiveness

Aysha hit Sylvester and ran but Sylvester caught her before she could get in the house. They were just playing but when Sylvester hit her she fell down and hurt her knee. She was mad at him because she said he hit her to hard and made her fall down. Sylvester said you hit me first it's not my fault that you fell down. Aysha didn't want to play with Sylvester anymore. Sylvester told her he was sorry but she wouldn't listen and she didn't want to talk to him. She told his mom that he hit her and made her fall down and hurt herself. His mom said he said he was sorry just forgive him; go play and keep your hands to yourself. It is not good to stay mad at someone for a long time. It could make you sick and you will never be happy. You must learn how to give it to God and let go of it.

Dear God, I have been hurt by _____ (say their name if you know it) and I forgive him/her with your help. I thank You for peace and forgiveness in my heart. Bless him/her and give them peace in Jesus' name. Amen!

"And whenever you stand praying, if you have anything against anyone, forgive him, that your Father in heaven may also forgive you your trespasses. 26 But if you do not forgive, neither will your Father in heaven forgive your trespasses."   Mark 11:25, 26

Let all bitterness, wrath, anger, clamor and evil speaking be put away from you with all malice. And be kind to one another, tenderhearted, forgiving one another, even as God in Christ forgave you. Ephesians 4:31, 32

People do things that hurt others all the time. But we must forgive them and go on with our lives. Some times they do it on purpose and some times it is an accident. Either way you must forgive them and go on. Some times adults take children from their families and hurt or kill the child. The family has to forgive that person and go on with their lives. A man shot and killed my son I forgive him and pray that he forgives himself for doing something so cruel. If all you do is sit and think about the bad things that happen to you. You will never get out and enjoy life you have to forgive that person. You have to let go of that horrible feeling and forgive whoever hurt you.

Confession

I forgive those who have hurt me just like God has forgiven me for the things I have done wrong. If we confess our sins, He is faithful and just to forgive us our sins and to cleanse us from all unrighteousness.   1 John 1:9

Take Care of Others and God will take care of you

**Give, and it will be given to you: good measure, pressed down, shaken together, and running over will be put into your bosom. For with the same measure that you use, it will be measured back to you.
            Luke 6:38**

**And Jesus increased in wisdom and stature, and in favor with God and men.
Luke 2:52**

**Let each of you look out not only for his own interests, but also for the interests of others.
Philippians 2:4**

So let each one give as he purposes in his heart, not grudgingly or of necessity for God loves a cheerful giver. 2 Corinthians 9:7

**And God is able to make all grace abound toward you, that you, always having all sufficiency in all things, may have abundance for every good work.
2 Corinthians 9:8**

**Save now, I pray, O Lord. O Lord, I pray send now prosperity.
Psalm 118:25**

Lying

Joe came home from school and he was hungry but dinner wasn't ready yet. So he ask his Mom could he have a cookie until dinner get ready. She told him no because dinner was almost done. Joe got a cookie anyway because Mon was in the other room and he ran up the stairs so she wouldn't see him eating it. When he finished eating it Mom called him to come eat but he wasn't hungry any more. He came down stairs and sat at the table but he didn't eat his food. His Mom asked him why he wasn't eating. He told her he wasn't hungry now. Mom asked why wasn't he hungry anymore did he eat a cookie after she told him not to. He told her no he didn't eat a cookie he just wasn't hungry. Mom said I am going to check the cookie jar because I know how many cookies was in there so you better be telling the truth or you are going to be in trouble. He said ok I did eat a cookie after you told me not to I am sorry but I was really hungry. His Mom told him he couldn't go out side because he lied to her. She told him it is not good to lie because no one will believe anything you say. Your lie could hurt a person when they find out you are lying so don't lie period. You did what I told you not to do the same thing Adam did when God told him not to eat from the tree and he ate from the tree anyway. Adam disobeyed God and that cause everyone to be born in sin, everyone was born separted from God. Now because of you no one in the house will get a cookie because I am going to get rid of all the cookies so you can't do it again.

A false witness will not go unpunished and he who speaks lies will not escape.
Proverbs 19:5

A righteous man hates lying but a wicked man is loathsome and comes to shame.
Proverbs 13:5

You are of your father the devil, and the desires of your father you want to do. He was a murderer from the beginning, and does not stand in the truth, because there is no truth in him. When he speaks a lie, he speaks from his own resources, for he is a liar and the father of it.
John 8:44

Confessions

I am the righteousness of God and I don't tell lies
I am a new creation old things have passed away all things have become new

God supply all your need!

But my God shall supply all your need according to His riches in glory by Christ Jesus.
Philippians 4:19

And God is able to make all grace abound toward you, that you, always having all sufficiency in all things, may have an abundance for every good work.   2 Corinthians 9:8

Now to Him who is able to do exceedingly abundantly above all that we ask or think, according to the power that works in us,   Ephesians 3:20

Blessed be the God and Father of our Lord Jesus Christ, who has blessed us with every spiritual blessing in the heavenly places in Christ,   Ephesians 1:3

And you shall remember the Lord your God, for it is He who gives you power to get wealth that He may establish His covenant which He sword to your fathers as it is this day.
Deuteronomt 8:18

Delight yourself also in the Lord and He shall give you the desires of your heart.
Psalm 37:4

If you are willing and obedient you shall eat the good of the land. Isaiah 1:19
For you know the grace of our Lord Jesus Christ, that though He was rich, yet for your sakes He became poor, that you through His poverty might become rich.   2 Corinthians 8:9

Stealing

Brea was visiting a friend they were laughing and having a good time together. He friend showed her some beautiful ear rings that her grandma had given her for her birthday. She told Brea she didn't like the ear rings and she never wore them. She put the ear rings back in the box and stuck them in drawer. They left her room and went into the kitchen to make some sandwiches.

Brea said she had to go to the bathroom and left the kitchen. She went back into the bedroom and took the box out of the drawer. She took the ear rings out of the box and put them in her pocket. Then she put the box back in the drawer and went to the bathroom. She knew taking the ear rings wasn't right but she told herself that her friend didn't like them and she didn't want them. So she went back into the kitchen and made her sandwich and they laughed and talk until it was time for Brea to go home.

Brea's dad picked her up from her friend's house. Brea told her bye and that she would see her at school tomorrow. When her friend got to school the next day she asked Brea did she know where her ear rings was. Because her mom wanted them but when she looked in the box they were not there and she know she put them back in the box in the drawer.
Brea started to lie and say she didn't know but she told her the truth because she didn't want to lose her friendship. They had been friends for a long time and she knew she should have never taken the ear rings in the first place. So she told her she had the ear rings at home and that she would bring them to her when got out of school. Her friend asked her why did she take them she would have let her wear them if she had asked her for them.

Brea said, you said you didn't like and that you had never wore them so I thought you didn't want them. Her friend they were from my grandma so I did want them I would have wore them when grandma came to visit. Brea told her she was sorry for taken them without asking she said she would never do anything like that again. Brea asked her to forgive her for taking her ear rings/ She hugged Brea and told her that she forgive her stealing her ear rings. Do not steal from me again just ask me can you borrow it for little while.

The thief does not come except to steal, and to kill, and to destroy. I (Jesus) have come that they may have life, and that they may have it more abundantly.   John 10:10

Let him who stole steal no longer, but rather let him labor, working with his hands what is good, that he may have something to give him who has need.   Ephesians 4:28

It is not nice to steal other people things. The word of God says that God supply all your need according to His riches in glory by Christ Jesus. (Philippians 4:19) God did not tell you to steal what you need or want. The word says to believe what the word says and to act like it is so. The word of God also says to delight yourself in God and He will give you the desire of your heart. (Psalm 37:4) You don't have to steal believe and trust God and He will take care of you.

Confessions

God supply all my need according to His riches in glory by Christ Jesus
I delight myself in the Lord and He gives me the desires of my heart
Greater is He who is in me than he (stealing, lying) that is in the world

Behold! I (Jesus) give you the authority to trample on serpents and scorpions and over all the power of the enemy and nothing shall by any means hurt you.   Luke 10:19

Your enemy is anything or anyone that is against you and trying to stop you from doing what God has told you to do. It is a person who is trying to hurt you and speak evil negative things over you.

Everyone is not your friend if they are trying to talk you into doing something that is not right they are not your friend they are a enemy. If they are calling you nasty names they are not your friend they are your enemy. A true friend loves you they want to see you to do good and what is right. They don't want to see you get hurt or see you hurt someone else.

A man who has friends must himself be friendly, but there is a friend who sticks closer than a brother.   Proverbs 18:24

When people say bad or negative words about you, you say what God says about you. Look in the mirror and tell yourself this. Say this to yourself over and over again until you believe it.

I am made in the image and likeness of God.

I am special

I am smart

I am beautiful or handsome

I can do all things through Christ

I am loved Jesus loves me He died for me

As a man thinks in he heart so is he.

Think and say good things about yourself.

I believe all things are possible to me.

I delight myself in the Lord and He gives me the desires of my heart.

I am fearfully and wonderfully made by God

I have the mind of Christ and the wisdom of God.

I am wise God teaches me all things.

I Know I Can

Aysha always told herself that she couldn't do anything and what she could do she couldn't do it right. Every time someone says she can she says she "can't." She was so use to being told "you can't do that" now she really believes that she can't do anything.

Aysha wants to be a cheerleader but she is afraid to try out. Because she believes she can't do it but she really can if she would only believe she could. She tried before but she was so nervous she didn't make it and she was very upset.

Brea told her that she could be a good cheerleader if she would only believe that she could be. Brea said you can do anything through Christ if only you would believe it. You have to believe in yourself and know that you can do it. God made each one of us special in our own way. You don't have to be afraid or nervous because Jesus is always with you. All things are possible to you if you believe it is. (Mark 9:23)

So Aysha tried out again but this time she practiced really hard and she believed in herself. She knew she could do it, she was not afraid or nervous, she had a lot of confidence in herself. She did a very good job and she got to be a cheerleader. She told Brea thank you for believing in her. They celebrated Aysha becoming a cheerleader.

Whatever you desire to do, don't be afraid to do it. You can do whatever you believe you can do. If you tell yourself you can't then you want even try. You can do it if you believe you can. Get out there and do it tell yourself you can do it.

Confessions:

I can do all things through Christ Jesus who strengthens me. Philippians 4:13

As I think so am I. Proverbs 23:7

I believe all things are possible to me. Mark 9:23

I am more than a conqueror Romans 8:37

I am victorious. 1 Corinthians 15:57

Renew Your Mind to the Word of God

I beseech you therefore, brethren, by the mercies of God, that you present your bodies a living sacrifice, holy, acceptable to God, *which* **is your reasonable service. And do not be conformed to this world, but be transformed by the renewing of your mind, that you may prove what is that good and acceptable and perfect will of God.   Romans 12:1,2**

If then you were raised with Christ, seek those things which are above, where Christ is, sitting at the right hand of God. ² Set your mind on things above, not on things on the earth. ³ For you died, and your life is hidden with Christ in God.   Colossians 3:1-3

For the weapons of our warfare are not carnal but mighty in God for pulling down strongholds, ⁵casting down arguments and every high thing that exalts itself against the knowledge of God, bringing every thought into captivity to the obedience of Christ   2 Corinthians 10:4, 5

Tithing

Give God what belongs to Him a tenth of everything you get. A tenth of your time and a tenth of your money. Give your time by reading, studying and confessing the word of God. Give by volunteering to help others. Give your money to the church to help pay bills, to help feed the hungry, the poor and the needy. Ask God who you should give money to and how much should you give? JUST GIVE! "Will a man rob God?
Yet you have robbed Me! But you say, In what way have we robbed You?'In tithes and offerings. ⁹ You are cursed with a curse, For you have robbed Me, *Even* this whole nation.¹⁰ Bring all the tithes into the storehouse, That there may be food in My house, And try Me now in this," Says the LORD of hosts, If I will not open for you the windows of heaven And pour out for you *such* blessing That *there will* not *be room* enough to receive it. 11 "And I will rebuke the devourer for your sakes, So that he will not destroy the fruit of your ground, Nor shall the vine fail to bear fruit for you in the field,"
Says the LORD of hosts;

My Personal Space

Everyone has their own personal space and gets uncomfortable when someone steps into it. If someone is touching you in places they shouldn't be touching you. You need to tell it to someone, don't be afraid and if you are you really need to tell. It doesn't make any difference who it is tell it. You didn't do anything wrong the person who touched you is the one who did something wrong. It is not right for them to touch you and you shouldn't be shame just tell it. The first time they touch you the wrong way tell it don't wait. Be strong and tell it or if you know that someone else is going through this and they are afraid to tell you tell it.

Be strong in the Lord and in the power of His might. Put on the whole armor of God. Ephesians 6:10

I can do all things through Christ who strengthen me.   Philippians 4:13

Clara's mom had a new boyfriend, he seemed like a really nice guy. He played games eith us all the time. I had two brothers and one sister. I have a big brother who is eleven, a a little brother that is six and a little sister that is eight. I am ten and I am in the fifth grande. We pop popcorn and watch movies with my mom and her boyfriend. One day my mom had to go to work in the evening time she usually work while we are in school. She went to work and left us with her boyfriend. We played games for awhile and then we watched a movie. Mom's boyfriend went into the other room and then he called me and tole me to come here he wanted to show me something. So I went into the room to see what he wanted and he we are going to play a game just me and you. You can't tell anyone else about this game it's between me and you. He do you promise not to tell anyone else and I said ok I promise not to tell anyone else. I asked how do we play the game and he said you have to pulled down your pants and I will show you. I said, What? Why? I don't want to pull down my pants, I don't want to play this game. He said you will like this game you have to try it to see if you like it. She said no I don't want to play I going back and finished watching the movie. When she went to open the door he grab her and put his hand over her mouth so she couldn't scream for help. He told her I just want you to see what the game is going to be like. He put his hands down her pants and touch her on her private part. She tried to scream but he held her mouth real tight. Then he took her hand and made her touch his private part. He told her if you tell anyone I am going to

hurt you and your mom, your brothers and your sister. You promised that you wouldn't tell anyone. Then he laid he on the bed and got on top of her and she began to cry. He told her not

to cry he wasn't going to do anything to her he just wanted to know how the game goes and he let her go. She just off the bed and ran into the room where her sister and brothers were watching a movie. About time her mom came home she was in the bed she was afraid to go to sleep because she didn't want him to come into their room. He might do her little sister the same way and she didn't want that. The next day she was really quiet and mom asked was she feeling alright and she said yes she was fine. Mom told them she had to work again in the evening instead of the morning. Clara said can't we go over to our aunt's house to stay until it is time to go to bed. Mom said no her boyfriend was going to be there they could stay with him. Clara told she didn't want to and mom asked her "Why?" I thought all of you like being with him and everyone said we do. We have a lot of fun with him playing games and watching mvies. Mom said, "OK" all of you can stay here then. Clara looked at her mom's boyfriend and rolled her eyes because she was hoping he didn't want to play that game again. When mom left they went into the TV room and picked out a movie to watch and went into the kitchen to pop some popcorn. Everything was going fine it was almost time to go to bed and he hadn't called her into the other room. But he got up and said I am going to grab someone and run off. He grab Clara and started running to the other room and she was screaming and holloring "NO" "Put me down I don't want to play." "I want to watch the movie" "NO" They all thought he was playing a game so they just up running and screaming the monster is going to get us "Hel[" clara was yelling help too but they weren't paying her any attention. He ran in the room and close the door and locked it. They ran to the door banging on it and yelling let her go you monster, let her go. Clara yelled "leave me alone I don't want to play your game. He told her she better be quiet and do what he says or he was going to hurt her and her sister and brothers. So she daid there and cried. He started pulling down her pants and she yelled "NO" stop it. He put his hands on her private part and he rubbed his private part on her and she yelled and cried. Then she her the other kids yelling mommy, mommy you came home early. He told her to get up and get her pants on and hurry up. Her mom knocked on the door and tried to open it but she couldn't because it was locked. She said what are you doing in there. The yelled his a monster and he took Clara in there to make her a monster too. Mom said open the door and he opened the door and Clara ran out and grabbed her mommy and said I am glad you are here. She why have you been crying and wiped away her tears. Her boyfriend she didn't want to play and I made her play anyway so she started crying. She's alright your alright Clara right and Clara said no he touch me and made me touch him . I told him I didn't want to play that game with him and he made me play anyway. He said he was going to hurt you; my brothers and my little sister. I don't want him here anymore mommy, Please make him lieave. Mommy told the kids to go finish watching the movie and she told him to get out and don't come back or she was going to call the police on him. So he got his stuff and moved out. Mom called the police on him anyway because she didn't want him to do another little girl the way he had did her little girl.

Watch who you allow to be around your children at all times!

Death of a Loved One!

Having a love one die is so hard to explain to a child. The scriptures show us to be absent from the body is to be present with the Lord. I believe God warns the person before they die. To me He wouldn't be a just God if He didn't. If you know God then you know that He is a just God. So I believe He warm us by telling us something is going to happen or He tells the person to come on home with Him. When it is a sudden death that its really hard to take. It helps to have a relationship with God so that you can talk to Him about it. My son was shot and killed I believe my son was warned and my son chose to be in that place anyway. Maybe he didn't understand the warning and maybe he did. I will ask him when I go to heaven. But I did ask God and He said He warned my son and my son chose to go. God didn't tell us because we would have prayed against my son wishes. He wanted to go we didn't want him to go so we would have prayed against his wishes.But the Lord put His loving arms around me and heoped me to handle losing my son. We must remember that are love ones belong to God and not us. He gave us our children but we have to turn them back over to Him. He can take better care of them then we can. He is must wiser and He knows all things and He can protect them better then we can. We knows that He loves us because He gave His only begotten Son for us so we could get on fellowshipping with Him. The blood of Jesus set of free and set us and put us in right standing with God. The Lord is on our side He is not against us.

Adam disobeyed God and ate from the tree God had told him not to eat from brought death to everyone born after him. Adam lived to be 930 years old because he did not know how to die. God made us to live forever with Him. Now everyone must die if you have asked Jesus to come live in your heart you will go to heaven to be with Jesus. We will see our love ones again and then we will never die again. We will live forever with Jesus.

I shall not die, but live and declare the works of the Lord. Psalm 118:17

So we are always confident, knowing that while we are at home in the body we are absent from the Lord. For we walk by faith not by sight. We are confident yes, well pleased rather to be absent from the body and to be present with the Lord.   2 Corinthians 5:6-8

The last enemy to be destroyed is death. 1 Corinthians 15:26

But we see Jesus, who was made a little lower than the angels, for the suffering of death crowned with glory and honor, that He, by the grace of God, might taste death for everyone. Hebrews 2:9

Jesus died on the cross for everyone taking all of our sins, sickness, disease, poverty, lack and death. Our punishment for disobeying God was death the sin brought on sickness, disease, poverty and lack. Jesus took it all when He died on the cross. When we ask Jesus to come live in our hearts He gives us the victory over sin, sickness, disease, poverty, lack and death. He gives us divine health, divine wealth and eternal life. It is up to us to believe and confess that we have good health, wealth and eternal life. We have to say it, believe it and act like it is so. Jesus has already won it for us by dying on the cross for us and He came back to life taking the victory over death. Rather we believe it or act like it is true it is true. He won it for us and gave us the victory over all of it. But our bodies still want to live the old way by getting sick and dying. We have to teach our bodies to obey the word of God and live a healthy wealthy long life. Jesus already took it all for us so we don't have to be sick and poor we must make our bodies believe that. We died so God can give us a new body so that we can live with Him forever. The bodies we have now can't live with God because it wants to do the wrong things instead of the right things. We have to teach our bodies to live the way God planned for us to live before Adam sinned. God loves us so much that He gave His Son Jesus to die for us. Jesus loves us so much that He came from heaven to died for us. He gave us the victory and He gave us His Holy Spirit to live in us so we could live a victorious life.

God does not cause death or bring death to anyone. God has taken three people and He took them alive. Enoch, Elijah and Jesus went to heaven alive they did not die.

Genesis 5:21-24 Enoch lived sixty-five years and begot Methuselah. After he begot Methuselah, Enoch walked with God three hundred years and had sons and daughters. So all the days of Enoch were three hundred and sixty-five years. And Enoch walked with God and he was not, for God took him.

2 Kings 2:9-11 And so it was, when they had crossed over, that Elijah said to Elisha, Ask! What may I do for you, before I am taken away from you? Elisha said, Please let a double portion of your spirit be upon me. So he said, You have asked a hard thing. Nevertheless, if you see me when I am take from you, it shall be so for you; but if not it shall not be so. Then it happened, as they continued on and talked, that suddenly a chariot of fire appeared with horses of fire and separated the two of them and Elijah went up by a whirlwind into heaven.

Mark 16:19 So then after the Lord had spoken to them, He was received up into heaven and sat down at the right hand of God.

Luke 24:50-53 And He led them out as far as Bethany and He lifted up His hands and blessed them. Now it came to pass, while He blessed them that He was parted from them and carried up into heaven. And they worshiped Him and returned to Jerusalem with great joy and were continually in the temple praising and blessing God. Amen.

Acts 1:9-11 Now when He had spoken these things, while they watched, He was taken up and a cloud received Him out of their sight. And while they looked steadfastly toward heaven as He went up, behold, two men stood by them in white apparel. Who also said, Men of Galilee, why do you stand gazing up into heaven? This same Jesus, who was taken up from you into heaven, will so come in like manner as you saw Him go into heaven.

We have the victory over death because Jesus overcame death. He died and then He got up taking the victory over death. Jesus will never die again. When Jesus come back to the earth to destroy the devil for good we will be given a new body that will never die. We have the victory now but we have to train our bodies to be the way God created us to be before sin came into the world. Our bodies want to live the sinful way not God's way. We were created to live forever. We must control our bodies with the word of God and our recreated spirit. Our spirits our recreated when we confess Jesus as our Lord and Savior.

2 Corinthians 5: [17] Therefore, if anyone *is* in Christ, *he* is a new creation; old things have passed away; behold, all things have become new.

Crown with Loving kindness & Tender Mercies

Bless the Lord O my soul and all that is with in me. Bless His holy name! Bless the Lord O my soul and forget not all His benefits, Who forgives all my inquities, Who heals all my diseases, Who redeems my life from destruction, Who crown me with loving kindness and tender mercies, Who satisfies my mouth with good things so that my youth will be renewed like the eagle's.

For You have made him a little lower than the angels, And You have crowned him with glory and honor.   Psalm 8:5

Confessions

Say these three times a day.

By Jesus' stripes I am healed.
1 Peter 2:24

God sent His word and healed me and delivered me from my destruction.
Psalm 107:20

Jesus took all my infirmities and all my sickness.
Matthew 8:17

I can do all things through Christ who strengthen me.
Philippians 4:13

Greater is He who is in me than he who is in the world.
1 John 4:4

God did not give me the spirit of fear, but of power, of love and of a sound mind.
1 Timothy 1:7

God supply all my need according to His riches in glory by Christ Jesus.
Philippians 4:19

I delight myself in the Lord and He gives me the desires of my heart.
Psalm 37:4

If God is for me who can be against me?
Romans 8:31

I am a child of God, I am a heir of God and a joint heir with Christ.
Romans 8:

I am made in the image and likeness of God.
Genesis 1:26

I am more than a conqueror through Christ who loves me.
Romans 8

I am the righteousness of God through Christ Jesus.
Romans 5:21

I am victorious through Christ. I am a winner.
1 Corinthians 15:57

I am an overcome I overcome by the blood of the Lamb and the word of my testimony
Revelation 12:11

I have the mind of Christ and the wisdom of God.

No evil shall befall me nor shall any plague (sickness, poverty) come near my dwelling.
Psalm 91:10

No weapon formed against me shall prosper. Any tongue that rises against me shall be shown to be in the wrong. Isaiah 55:17

I am the head and not the tail I am above only and not beneath.
Deuteronomy 28:13

I am blessed coming in and blessed going out.
Deuteronomy 28:6

I let the peace of God rule in my heart and mind and I refuse to worry about anything.
Colossians 3:15   Philippians 4:6

I cast all my cares on Jesus because He cares for me.
1 Peter 5:7

God gave me the power, the ability, the wisdom to get wealth.
Deuteronomy 8:18

I believe all things are possible to me.
Mark 9:23

With God all things are possible.
Mark

I give and it is given to me good measure, press down, shaken together and running over.
Luke 6:38

The Lord is on my side Who shall I fear? What can man do to me
Psalm

Protection

He who dwells in the secret place of the Most High shall abide under the shadow of the Almighty. I will say of the Lord, He is my refuge and my fortress; My God, in Him I will trust. Surely He shall deliver me from the snare of the fowler and from the perilous pestilence. He shall cover me with His feathers and under His wings I shall take refuge; He truth shall be my shield and buckler. I shall not be afraid of the terror by night nor of the arrow that flies by day, nor of the destruction that lays waste at noonday. A thousand may fall at my side and ten thousand at my right hand but it shall not come near me. Only with my eyes shall I look and see the reward of the wicked. Because I have made the Lord, who is my refuge even the Most High my dwelling place. No eil shall befall me nor shall any plague come near my dwelling for He shall give His angels charge over me to keep me in all my ways. In their hands they shall bear me up lest I dash my foot against a stone. I shall tread upon the lion and the serpent I shall trample underfoot. Because He has set His love upon me therefore He will deliver me. I will set him on high because he has known my name. He shall call upon me and I will answer him. I will be with him in trouble; I will deliver him and honor him, with long life I will satisfy him and show him my salvation.   Psalm 91

Confess Jesus as your Lord and Savior

If you have never confess Jesus as your Lord and you want to just say this prayer out loud.

12 Therefore, just as through one man sin entered the world, and death through sin, and thus death spread to all men, because all sinned—

17 For if by the one man's offense death reigned through the one, much more those who receive abundance of grace and of the gift of righteousness will reign in life through the One, Jesus Christ.)   Romans 5:12, 17

If you confess with your mouth the Lord Jesus and believe in your heart that God has raised Him from the dead you will be saved. For with the heart one believes unto righteousness and with the mouth confession is made unto salvation. Romans 10:9, 10

Dear God, I believe Jesus died for my sins and now He is with you. I turn my life over to Jesus and ask Him to come live in my heart. I believe that I have what I have asked for and I am now a child of God and Jesus lives in me. Thank You! In Jesus' name. Amen!

God Uses Kids Too!

And it shall come to pass in the last days says God, that I will pour out of My Spirit on all flesh. Your sons and your daughters shall prophesy. Your young men shall see visions. Your old men shall dream dreams. Acts 2:17

God is not a man that He should lie, nor a son of man that He should repent. Has He said and will He not do? Or has He spoken and will He not make it good? Numbers 23:19

CPSIA information can be obtained
at www.ICGtesting.com
Printed in the USA
LVIC071422130313
324133LV00002B